Insights into Financial Frauds and Scams

C. P. Kumar
Reiki Healer & Author
Roorkee - 247667, India

Copyright © 2024 C. P. Kumar

All rights reserved.

No part of this book may be reproduced or transmitted in any form or by any means, electronic or mechanical, including photocopying, recording, or by any information storage and retrieval system, without permission in writing from the author.

Disclaimer

While every effort has been made to ensure the accuracy and completeness of the content in this book, the author cannot guarantee that the information contained herein is error-free, up-to-date, or suitable for every individual circumstance.

The author shall not be held liable or responsible for any errors or omissions in the content of the book, nor for any damages, or losses that may arise from any actions taken based upon the suggestions or contents presented in the book.

Readers are advised to use their own judgment and discretion in applying the information provided in this book, and to consult with qualified professionals before taking any action based on the contents of this book. The author disclaims any and all liability or responsibility for any actions taken or not taken based on the information contained in this book.

DEDICATION

To all those who strive for transparency, integrity, and fairness in the realm of finance,

This book is dedicated to the vigilant souls who relentlessly pursue truth amidst the shadows of deceit. Your commitment to unraveling the intricacies of financial frauds and scams serves as a beacon of hope for investors and regulators alike.

May your unwavering dedication inspire a future where trust reigns supreme, and where the principles of honesty and accountability illuminate every transaction.

In memory of those whose lives have been adversely impacted by financial malfeasance, and in honor of those who tirelessly work to prevent its recurrence.

This dedication stands as a testament to the collective effort needed to safeguard our financial systems and protect the dreams of millions.

With deepest gratitude,

C. P. Kumar

CONTENTS

PREFACE

Financial fraud and scams represent a dark underbelly of the global economy, threatening the trust and stability upon which financial markets and institutions are built. From intricate Ponzi schemes to sophisticated cybersecurity breaches, the landscape of financial malfeasance is vast and ever-evolving. In the wake of these fraudulent activities lie shattered lives, ruined investments, and tarnished reputations.

This book, "Insights into Financial Frauds and Scams", embarks on a journey through the murky waters of deceit, manipulation, and exploitation that plague the world of finance. Through its pages, readers will delve into the multifaceted nature of financial fraud, gaining a deeper understanding of its mechanisms, consequences, and the challenges it poses to investors, regulators, and society at large.

The chapters within this volume serve as illuminating signposts, guiding readers through various facets of financial fraud and deception. We begin with an exploration of the landscape of financial fraud, providing a foundational understanding of its scope and complexity. From there, we navigate through the treacherous terrain of insider trading, securities fraud, and market manipulation, unraveling the webs of deceit that undermine investor trust and market integrity.

As we journey further, we confront the insidious nature of accounting fraud, churning, and unauthorized trading, shedding light on the deceptive practices that erode the financial well-being of individuals and organizations alike. We delve into the intricate structures of pyramid schemes, Ponzi schemes, and high-yield investment scams, uncovering the illusions of easy wealth that lure unsuspecting victims into financial ruin.

In the digital age, the threat of financial fraud extends into the realm of cyberspace, where identity theft, phishing scams, and cybersecurity breaches pose formidable challenges to individuals and institutions alike. Moreover, the shadowy world of money laundering casts a long and sinister shadow over the global financial system, perpetuating crime and corruption on a massive scale.

Amidst these challenges, regulatory agencies and enforcement authorities stand as bulwarks against the tide of financial malfeasance, navigating a complex landscape of legal frameworks, investigative techniques, and international cooperation. Yet, despite their efforts, the battle against financial fraud remains ongoing, demanding vigilance, innovation, and resilience from all stakeholders.

Embedded within these pages are not only tales of deception and betrayal but also insights into strategies for protection and prevention. From tips for safeguarding investments to best practices for navigating the digital frontier, readers will find practical guidance for fortifying themselves against the threat of financial fraud.

As we embark on this journey together, let us remain vigilant and informed, recognizing that the fight against financial fraud is a collective endeavor - one that requires awareness, integrity, and a steadfast commitment to upholding the principles of transparency and accountability. Through knowledge and awareness, we empower ourselves to navigate the complexities of the financial world with confidence and resilience.

May this book serve as a beacon of light amidst the shadows, illuminating the path towards a future where trust, integrity, and ethical conduct reign supreme in the realm of finance.

C. P. Kumar
Reiki Healer, Blogger & Author
Former Scientist 'G', National Institute of Hydrology
Roorkee - 247667, India
Web: https://www.angelfire.com/nh/cpkumar/virgo.html

Financial fraud represents a pervasive threat to individuals, businesses, and economies worldwide. It encompasses a range of illicit activities designed to deceive, manipulate, or misrepresent financial information for personal gain or to the detriment of others. Understanding the landscape of financial fraud is essential for safeguarding against its pernicious effects and maintaining the integrity of financial systems. In this chapter, we embark on a comprehensive exploration of financial fraud, examining its various forms, underlying mechanisms, and the profound impact it has on stakeholders.

The Nature of Financial Fraud

Financial fraud manifests in diverse forms, each characterized by distinct methodologies and objectives. At its core, financial fraud entails the intentional deception or manipulation of financial transactions, statements, or instruments for unlawful purposes. From insider trading to pyramid schemes, perpetrators exploit vulnerabilities in financial systems to perpetrate their schemes and illicit activities.

Exploring the Motivations Behind Financial Fraud

Understanding the motivations driving individuals and organizations to engage in financial fraud is crucial for comprehending its prevalence and dynamics. While financial gain often serves as a primary incentive, other factors such as power, prestige, and the desire to conceal underlying financial weaknesses may also drive fraudulent behavior. Moreover, the allure of perceived opportunities for quick wealth and the pressure to meet unrealistic performance targets can incentivize individuals to resort to fraudulent practices.

The Impact of Financial Fraud

The ramifications of financial fraud extend far beyond its immediate victims, reverberating throughout economies and societies. Investors may suffer substantial financial losses, eroding trust in financial markets and institutions. Moreover, the broader economy may experience disruptions, reduced investor confidence, and diminished economic growth prospects as a result of pervasive fraudulent activities. In addition to financial losses, victims of financial fraud often endure significant emotional distress, reputational damage, and legal repercussions.

Key Factors Contributing to Financial Fraud

Several factors contribute to the proliferation of financial fraud, ranging from systemic vulnerabilities to cultural and regulatory shortcomings. Rapid technological advancements, complex financial instruments, and global interconnectedness have created new avenues for fraudsters to exploit. Furthermore, lax regulatory oversight, inadequate enforcement mechanisms, and cultural norms that prioritize profit over ethical conduct can facilitate fraudulent activities and undermine the integrity of financial systems.

The Evolution of Financial Fraud in the Digital Age

The advent of digital technologies has transformed the landscape of financial fraud, presenting both opportunities and challenges for stakeholders. Cybercriminals leverage sophisticated tactics such as identity theft, phishing scams, and cybersecurity breaches to infiltrate financial systems and perpetrate fraudulent activities. As digital transactions become increasingly prevalent, the risk of cyber-enabled financial fraud continues to escalate, necessitating robust cybersecurity measures and heightened vigilance.

The Role of Psychology in Financial Fraud

Psychological factors play a pivotal role in the perpetration and perpetuation of financial fraud. Perpetrators often exploit cognitive biases, emotional vulnerabilities, and social dynamics to manipulate victims and conceal their illicit activities. Understanding the psychological mechanisms underlying fraudulent behavior can inform prevention strategies and empower individuals to recognize and resist fraudulent schemes.

The Importance of Detection and Prevention

Detecting and preventing financial fraud require a multifaceted approach encompassing technological solutions, regulatory interventions, and heightened awareness among stakeholders. Implementing robust internal controls, conducting regular audits, and fostering a culture of transparency and accountability are essential components of effective fraud prevention strategies. Moreover, leveraging advanced analytics, artificial intelligence, and machine learning algorithms can enhance detection capabilities and mitigate the risk of financial fraud.

Conclusion

Financial fraud represents a formidable challenge confronting individuals, businesses, and societies in an increasingly interconnected and technologically driven world. By gaining a deeper understanding of the landscape of financial fraud, its underlying dynamics, and the mechanisms driving fraudulent behavior, stakeholders can better equip themselves to combat this pervasive threat. Through collaborative efforts, enhanced regulatory oversight, and a commitment to ethical conduct, we can strive to safeguard the integrity of financial systems and foster trust and confidence in global markets.

In subsequent chapters, we will delve into specific forms of financial fraud, examining their mechanics, consequences, and regulatory responses. From insider trading to money laundering, each chapter will offer valuable insights into the intricacies of financial fraud and equip readers with the knowledge and tools needed to navigate this complex and ever-evolving landscape.

Introduction

In the intricate web of financial markets, where fortunes are made and lost in the blink of an eye, there exists a clandestine practice that undermines the integrity of fair trading: insider trading. The allure of gaining an unfair advantage by accessing non-public information has tempted many to engage in this illicit activity, despite its severe legal and ethical ramifications. Insider trading represents a critical issue in the realm of financial frauds and scams, shedding light on the darker facets of market operations and the urgent need for stringent regulatory measures.

Understanding Insider Trading

Insider trading occurs when individuals with privileged access to confidential, material information about a publicly traded company use that information to gain an unfair advantage in the securities markets. This privileged information can include forthcoming earnings announcements, mergers and acquisitions, regulatory decisions, or other events that could significantly impact a company's stock price. Armed with such knowledge, insiders can execute trades that yield substantial profits or avoid devastating losses, at the expense of uninformed investors.

Types of Insider Trading

Insider trading can take various forms, each presenting unique challenges for detection and enforcement.

1. Classic Insider Trading: This type involves corporate insiders, such as executives, directors, and employees, who trade securities based on material, non-public information. These insiders have a fiduciary duty to shareholders and are prohibited from exploiting their privileged position for personal gain.

2. Tipper-Tippee Trading: In this scenario, a corporate insider shares confidential information with an outsider, known as a "tippee", who then trades on the basis of that information. While the tippee may not have direct access to the insider information, they are still liable for insider trading if they knew or should have known that the tipper breached a duty by disclosing the information.

3. Misappropriation: This form of insider trading involves individuals who obtain confidential information through a relationship of trust and confidence, such as attorneys, accountants, or consultants, and then use that information for personal gain in the securities markets, even if they owe no fiduciary duty to the company whose stock is traded.

The Impact of Insider Trading

The ramifications of insider trading extend far beyond individual transactions, permeating the very foundation of fair and transparent markets.

1. Erosion of Investor Confidence: Insider trading erodes investor confidence in the fairness and integrity of the financial markets. When investors perceive that the game is rigged in favor of insiders, they may become reluctant to participate, leading to reduced liquidity and efficiency in the markets.

2. Distorted Market Efficiency: Insider trading distorts market efficiency by allowing insiders to exploit informational asymmetries for personal gain. This undermines the fundamental principle of price discovery, as stock prices may not accurately reflect all available information, impairing the allocation of capital and resource allocation in the economy.

3. Unequal Access to Opportunities: Insider trading perpetuates inequality by affording privileged individuals access to lucrative investment opportunities that are unavailable to ordinary investors. This exacerbates disparities in wealth and reinforces perceptions of a two-tiered financial system, where the rules are stacked in favor of the well-connected few.

Regulatory Framework and Enforcement

To combat insider trading and preserve market integrity, regulatory authorities have implemented a robust framework of laws and regulations.

1. Securities Exchange Act of 1934 (United States): The Securities Exchange Act of 1934 prohibits insider trading and empowers the Securities and Exchange Commission (SEC) to investigate and prosecute violations of insider trading laws. Section 10(b) and Rule 10b-5 of the Act prohibit fraudulent and deceptive practices in connection with the purchase or sale of securities.

2. Insider Trading and Securities Fraud Enforcement Act of 1988 (United States): This legislation enhanced penalties for insider trading violations and expanded the scope of liability to include individuals who tip material, non-public information to others, even if they do not personally trade on the information.

3. Regulation Fair Disclosure (Reg FD): **Reg FD (United States)** aims to promote fair and full disclosure of material information to all investors by prohibiting selective disclosure of material information to favored parties, such as analysts or institutional investors, without simultaneously disclosing the information to the public.

4. Enforcement Actions: **Regulatory authorities, including the SEC and Department of Justice, actively pursue insider trading cases through civil and criminal enforcement actions.** These actions may result in significant fines, disgorgement of ill-gotten gains, injunctions, and, in egregious cases, imprisonment for violators.

Challenges and Future Outlook

Despite efforts to combat insider trading, significant challenges persist in detecting and deterring illicit activity.

1. Technological Complexity: **The proliferation of** electronic trading platforms and complex financial instruments has increased the complexity of insider trading investigations, requiring regulators to employ sophisticated surveillance techniques and data analytics to identify suspicious trading patterns.

2. Globalization of Markets: **In an era of globalized** markets, insider trading transcends national borders, posing challenges for cross-border enforcement and coordination among regulatory authorities with differing legal frameworks and jurisdictional constraints.

3. Regulatory Arbitrage: **Regulatory arbitrage allows** insider traders to exploit regulatory loopholes and jurisdictional differences to evade detection and

prosecution. Harmonizing regulatory standards and enhancing international cooperation are essential to address this challenge effectively.

4. Ethical Culture: Fostering a culture of integrity and ethical conduct within organizations is essential to prevent insider trading at its source. Companies must instill robust compliance programs, provide comprehensive training on insider trading laws and regulations, and cultivate a culture of transparency and accountability among employees.

Conclusion

Insider trading represents a pervasive threat to the integrity of financial markets, undermining investor confidence, distorting market efficiency, and perpetuating inequality. Through stringent regulatory oversight, enhanced enforcement efforts, and a commitment to ethical conduct, stakeholders can work together to combat insider trading and uphold the principles of fairness, transparency, and integrity in the global marketplace. As custodians of the financial system, we must remain vigilant in our efforts to root out illicit profiteering and preserve the trust and confidence of investors in the markets.

Introduction

Securities are financial instruments that represent an ownership position in a publicly-traded corporation (stock), a creditor relationship with a governmental body or a corporation (bond), or rights to ownership as represented by an option. They serve as a way for organizations to raise capital and for investors to potentially profit from their investments through dividends, interest, or capital gains.

In the vast landscape of financial markets, investors place their trust in the integrity of the system. However, lurking beneath the surface lies a pervasive threat: securities fraud. Securities fraud, a deceptive practice designed to manipulate markets or defraud investors, strikes at the heart of investor trust. This article delves into the intricate web of securities fraud, exploring its manifestations, consequences, and the imperative need for vigilance in safeguarding investor interests.

Understanding Securities Fraud

Securities fraud encompasses a spectrum of illicit activities orchestrated to deceive investors and manipulate financial markets. At its core, securities fraud involves the dissemination of false or misleading information to artificially inflate stock prices or lure unsuspecting investors into fraudulent schemes. From insider trading and accounting fraud to Ponzi schemes and pump-and-dump schemes, perpetrators employ diverse tactics to perpetrate fraud and exploit vulnerabilities within the financial ecosystem.

Insider Trading: The Betrayal of Trust

One of the most egregious forms of securities fraud is insider trading, wherein individuals with privileged access to non-public information exploit their position for personal gain. Armed with confidential corporate information, insiders engage in trades to capitalize on impending market movements, leaving ordinary investors at a distinct disadvantage. The insidious nature of insider trading not only undermines market integrity but also erodes investor confidence in the fairness of the system.

Accounting Fraud: Fabricating Financial Realities

Accounting fraud represents another pervasive threat to investor trust, involving the manipulation of financial statements to conceal underlying weaknesses or inflate corporate performance. Through creative accounting practices, companies misrepresent financial health, revenue streams, and asset values, painting a rosier picture than reality dictates. As unsuspecting investors rely on financial disclosures to inform investment decisions, the repercussions of accounting fraud can be far-reaching, culminating in substantial financial losses and shattered confidence.

Ponzi Schemes: Illusory Promises and Financial Ruin

The Ponzi scheme, immortalized by the infamous Charles Ponzi, epitomizes the deceitful allure of unsustainable investment schemes. Operating under the guise of legitimate ventures, Ponzi schemes promise extravagant returns to early investors, funded primarily through capital injections from subsequent investors. Yet, beneath the veneer of prosperity lies a precarious house of cards, destined to collapse once the influx of new investors wanes. As Ponzi schemes unravel, investors are left grappling with financial ruin, their trust betrayed by the false promises of unscrupulous operators.

Pump-and-Dump Schemes

Pump-and-dump schemes epitomize the art of market manipulation, leveraging hype and misinformation to artificially inflate stock prices before orchestrating a precipitous sell-off. Perpetrators disseminate misleading information or tout exaggerated claims to entice investors into buying shares of a particular stock, driving up demand and prices in the process. Once prices reach inflated levels, insiders swiftly unload their shares, reaping substantial profits while leaving unsuspecting investors holding devalued assets. Pump-and-dump schemes not only erode investor trust but also undermine the integrity of financial markets, perpetuating a cycle of deception and disillusionment.

Consequences of Securities Fraud

The ramifications of securities fraud extend far beyond financial losses, encompassing profound implications for investor confidence, market stability, and regulatory oversight. As investors grapple with the fallout of fraudulent schemes, trust in the fairness and transparency of financial markets diminishes, casting a shadow of doubt over the efficacy of regulatory safeguards. Moreover, the corrosive impact of securities fraud reverberates across the broader economy, eroding consumer confidence, stifling investment activity, and impeding economic growth.

Restoring Investor Trust

In the face of mounting threats posed by securities fraud, restoring investor trust demands a multifaceted approach encompassing robust regulatory enforcement, enhanced transparency, and investor education initiatives. Regulatory agencies must remain vigilant in detecting and prosecuting fraudulent activities, deploying sophisticated surveillance techniques and punitive measures to deter would-be perpetrators. Moreover, companies must prioritize transparency and accountability, fostering a culture of integrity and ethical conduct to mitigate the risk of fraud.

Investor education represents a linchpin in the fight against securities fraud, empowering individuals with the knowledge and tools necessary to navigate the complex landscape of financial markets. By fostering financial literacy and promoting awareness of common red flags, investors can better safeguard their interests and discern legitimate investment opportunities from fraudulent schemes. Collaboration between regulatory authorities, industry stakeholders, and advocacy groups is essential in fostering a culture of accountability and instilling confidence in the integrity of financial markets.

Conclusion

Securities fraud represents a formidable threat to investor trust, perpetuating a cycle of deception and disillusionment within financial markets. From insider trading and accounting fraud to Ponzi schemes and pump-and-dump schemes, the manifestations of securities fraud are diverse and insidious. Yet, through concerted efforts to enhance regulatory oversight, promote transparency, and bolster investor education, we can stem the tide of fraudulent activities and safeguard the interests of investors. In an era defined by volatility and uncertainty, the imperative to uphold the integrity of financial markets has never been more pressing. As stewards of investor trust, we must remain steadfast in our commitment to fostering fairness, transparency, and accountability within the financial ecosystem. Only then can we ensure that the promise of prosperity remains within reach for all participants in the global economy.

Introduction

In the intricate world of finance, market manipulation stands as a persistent threat, capable of destabilizing economies, eroding investor confidence, and distorting the integrity of financial markets. Defined as the deliberate attempt to interfere with the free and fair operation of market forces, market manipulation encompasses a wide array of tactics aimed at artificially influencing asset prices, trading volumes, and market perceptions. This article delves into the various tactics employed in market manipulation and explores the far-reaching consequences that ensue from such illicit activities.

Understanding Market Manipulation

At its core, market manipulation involves deceptive or fraudulent practices that create a false or misleading impression of market conditions. While regulatory bodies enact measures to curb such activities, perpetrators often devise ingenious schemes to circumvent detection and enforcement efforts. Understanding the motives behind market manipulation is crucial in comprehending its manifestations. Perpetrators may seek to inflate or deflate asset prices for personal gain, instigate panic-selling to profit from short positions, or artificially boost trading volumes to lure unsuspecting investors.

Tactics of Market Manipulation

1. Spoofing and Layering: Spoofing involves placing large buy or sell orders with the intention of canceling them

before execution, thereby creating a false impression of market demand or supply. Layering, a variant of spoofing, entails the placement of multiple orders at different price levels to manipulate market perceptions further. By swiftly withdrawing these orders once prices move in the desired direction, perpetrators capitalize on price fluctuations to execute profitable trades.

2. Pump and Dump Schemes: Commonly associated with penny stocks and cryptocurrencies, pump and dump schemes involve artificially inflating the price of an asset through misleading statements or promotional campaigns. Perpetrators purchase large quantities of the targeted asset at lower prices, disseminate favorable information to attract investors, and subsequently sell their holdings at inflated prices, leaving unsuspecting investors holding devalued assets.

3. Insider Trading: While not always classified as market manipulation per se, insider trading remains a prevalent form of illicit activity that undermines market integrity. Occurring when individuals trade securities based on material, non-public information, insider trading enables perpetrators to gain unfair advantages over other market participants. By exploiting their privileged access to confidential information, insiders distort market efficiency and compromise investor trust.

4. Churning: Churning involves excessive trading of an investor's account by a broker for the primary purpose of generating commissions, rather than serving the client's best interests. By executing a high volume of trades without regard for the investor's investment objectives or risk tolerance, unscrupulous brokers inflate trading costs and erode portfolio returns, thereby enriching themselves at the expense of their clients.

Consequences of Market Manipulation

The ramifications of market manipulation extend far beyond financial losses incurred by individual investors. By undermining the integrity and efficiency of financial markets, market manipulation erodes investor confidence, impairs capital allocation, and distorts price discovery mechanisms. The consequences of market manipulation can be broadly categorized into economic, regulatory, and reputational dimensions.

1. Economic Impact: Market manipulation disrupts the efficient allocation of capital by mispricing assets and deterring investment in legitimate enterprises. As investors lose confidence in the fairness and transparency of financial markets, capital flows may be diverted away from productive investments, hindering economic growth and innovation. Moreover, the misallocation of resources resulting from distorted market signals can lead to inefficiencies and market inefficiencies, exacerbating systemic risks.

2. Regulatory Response: Regulatory authorities bear the responsibility of safeguarding market integrity and preserving investor confidence through robust enforcement mechanisms. In response to evolving market dynamics and emerging threats, regulators continually refine and enhance their surveillance capabilities to detect and deter market manipulation. Enforcement actions, including civil penalties, disgorgement of ill-gotten gains, and criminal prosecutions, serve as deterrents to would-be perpetrators, signaling the severity of consequences for violating securities laws.

3. Reputational Damage: The revelation of market manipulation schemes tarnishes the reputation of implicated individuals, firms, and financial institutions, resulting in irreparable damage to their credibility and trustworthiness. In an era of heightened transparency and social media scrutiny, news of fraudulent activities spreads rapidly, amplifying reputational risks and precipitating public backlash. For financial institutions implicated in market manipulation scandals, the erosion of customer trust and investor confidence may precipitate long-term repercussions, including loss of market share and regulatory scrutiny.

Conclusion

Market manipulation represents a pervasive threat to the integrity and stability of financial markets, posing significant challenges to regulators, investors, and market participants alike. As financial markets become increasingly interconnected and technologically driven, the complexity and sophistication of market manipulation schemes continue to evolve, necessitating vigilant oversight and proactive enforcement measures. By enhancing transparency, promoting market integrity, and fostering a culture of compliance, stakeholders can mitigate the risks posed by market manipulation and uphold the principles of fairness and equity upon which financial markets are founded. Only through collective vigilance and unwavering commitment to ethical conduct can we safeguard the integrity and resilience of our global financial system.

Introduction

Financial fraud, particularly accounting fraud, represents a critical challenge to the integrity and stability of financial markets worldwide. Accounting fraud involves deliberate manipulation and misrepresentation of financial statements to deceive stakeholders about a company's financial performance and health. Among the various forms of accounting fraud, creative accounting and financial manipulation stand out as common tactics employed by unscrupulous individuals and organizations. This article delves into the intricacies of creative accounting and financial manipulation, exploring their methodologies, impacts, and preventive measures.

Understanding Creative Accounting

Creative accounting refers to the practice of exploiting the flexibility within accounting rules and regulations to present financial information in a favorable light, often at the expense of accuracy and transparency. While not all creative accounting practices are illegal per se, they can distort the true financial position of a company and mislead investors, creditors, and regulators. Common techniques associated with creative accounting include income smoothing, aggressive revenue recognition, off-balance-sheet financing, and understating liabilities.

Income smoothing involves manipulating financial results to create the illusion of stable and predictable earnings over time. Companies may artificially inflate or deflate revenues and expenses in different reporting periods to mask fluctuations and project a consistent growth trajectory. Aggressive revenue recognition entails recognizing revenue prematurely or inflating sales figures through fictitious transactions, channel stuffing, or improper accounting treatments. Off-balance-sheet financing involves keeping certain liabilities and assets off the balance sheet to improve financial ratios and mask financial risks. Such practices can include the use of special purpose entities (SPEs) or complex financial instruments to obscure debt obligations and commitments. *Special Purpose Entities* (SPEs) are legal entities created for a specific objective, often to isolate financial risk.

Implications of Creative Accounting

The pervasive use of creative accounting techniques can have far-reaching implications for stakeholders and the broader financial ecosystem. Investors relying on misrepresented financial statements may make flawed investment decisions, leading to financial losses and erosion of trust in capital markets. Lenders and creditors may extend credit based on inaccurate financial information, exposing themselves to heightened credit risks and potential defaults. Regulators tasked with ensuring transparency and accountability may struggle to detect and deter fraudulent activities, undermining the effectiveness of regulatory oversight mechanisms.

Furthermore, the erosion of investor confidence resulting from instances of creative accounting can have cascading effects on market dynamics and economic stability. Stock prices may experience volatility as investors reassess the true value of companies embroiled in accounting scandals. Reputational damage inflicted upon companies implicated in financial manipulation can tarnish their brand image and impair their ability to attract capital and talent. Moreover, the broader implications of creative accounting extend beyond individual companies to encompass systemic risks that threaten the stability and resilience of financial systems.

Detecting and Preventing Creative Accounting

Detecting and preventing creative accounting require a multifaceted approach that involves collaboration among regulators, auditors, corporate governance bodies, and investors. Regulators play a pivotal role in establishing and enforcing robust accounting standards and disclosure requirements aimed at enhancing transparency and integrity in financial reporting. Regulatory oversight mechanisms, such as periodic audits, inspections, and investigations, serve as deterrents against fraudulent practices and provide avenues for early detection and intervention.

Auditors, as independent third parties responsible for evaluating the accuracy and reliability of financial statements, play a critical role in detecting signs of creative accounting and financial manipulation. Through rigorous examination of financial records, internal controls, and audit trails, auditors can uncover discrepancies, irregularities, and red flags indicative of potential fraud. However, auditors must remain vigilant and exercise professional skepticism to resist undue influence or pressure from management to overlook irregularities or condone unethical practices.

Effective corporate governance practices, including the establishment of independent audit committees, the segregation of duties, and the implementation of robust internal controls, can serve as bulwarks against creative accounting and financial misconduct. By fostering a culture of transparency, accountability, and ethical conduct, companies can mitigate the risk of fraud and safeguard the interests of shareholders and other stakeholders. Moreover, proactive engagement and oversight by boards of directors and senior management are essential in promoting a culture of compliance and integrity throughout the organization.

Investors and financial analysts play a crucial role in holding companies accountable for their financial performance and disclosures. By conducting comprehensive due diligence, scrutinizing financial statements, and asking probing questions, investors can uncover inconsistencies and anomalies that may signal underlying financial manipulation. Moreover, active shareholder engagement, proxy voting, and shareholder activism can exert pressure on companies to adopt more transparent and accountable practices.

Conclusion

Creative accounting and financial manipulation represent grave threats to the integrity, transparency, and trustworthiness of financial reporting. While the pursuit of profitability and shareholder value is a legitimate objective for businesses, it must not come at the expense of ethical standards, regulatory compliance, and stakeholder trust. By fostering a culture of transparency, accountability, and ethical conduct, companies can fortify their defenses against fraudulent practices and enhance their long-term sustainability and resilience. Likewise, regulators, auditors, investors, and corporate governance bodies must remain vigilant and proactive in combating accounting fraud and upholding the integrity of financial markets. Only through collective vigilance and concerted action can we safeguard the integrity and stability of the global financial ecosystem against the scourge of creative accounting and financial manipulation.

Introduction

Financial markets are meant to be a bastion of trust and transparency, where investors confidently entrust their hard-earned capital to professionals who pledge to act in their best interests. However, beneath the veneer of legitimacy, there exists a dark underbelly of fraudulent practices that prey on investor trust. Among these insidious tactics are churning and unauthorized trading, two schemes that exploit investor trust for personal gain.

Understanding Churning

Churning refers to the excessive buying and selling of securities within a client's account by a broker, motivated primarily by generating commissions rather than serving the investor's best interests. The concept is straightforward: the more trades executed, the more commissions earned by the broker, regardless of whether those trades benefit the investor.

The Mechanics of Churning

Churning typically involves a broker exercising unauthorized control over a client's account, executing trades without the investor's consent or even knowledge. To conceal the scheme, brokers may provide falsified statements or misleading information that obfuscates the excessive trading activity. Meanwhile, investors remain unaware of the erosion of their portfolio value due to exorbitant transaction costs and potential losses incurred from ill-advised trades.

Psychological Manipulation and Exploitation

Churning thrives on exploiting investor psychology and trust. Brokers often cultivate relationships of dependency and authority, positioning themselves as knowledgeable advisors acting in the best interests of their clients. Through persuasive rhetoric and selective disclosure, brokers instill a false sense of confidence and security, thereby enabling the manipulation of client accounts for personal gain.

The Consequences of Churning

For investors, the consequences of churning can be financially devastating. Excessive trading generates substantial transaction costs that eat into investment returns, eroding capital over time. Moreover, frequent trading incurs tax liabilities, further diminishing net gains. Beyond financial losses, churning erodes trust in the financial system, tarnishing the reputation of legitimate brokers and undermining investor confidence.

Legal and Regulatory Framework

Recognizing the pernicious nature of churning, regulatory bodies have implemented safeguards to protect investors and maintain market integrity. Securities laws mandate that brokers adhere to fiduciary duties, acting solely in the best interests of their clients. Additionally, regulatory agencies such as the Securities and Exchange Commission (SEC) and the Financial Industry Regulatory Authority (FINRA) of United States of America enforce strict guidelines governing broker conduct and trading practices.

Detection and Prevention

Investors can mitigate the risk of falling victim to churning by remaining vigilant and informed. Regularly reviewing account statements and monitoring trading activity can help identify suspicious patterns indicative of churning. Establishing clear communication channels with brokers and setting investment objectives can deter unauthorized trading and promote transparency in client-broker relationships.

Unauthorized Trading

Unauthorized trading represents another form of exploitation wherein brokers execute trades without obtaining proper authorization from investors. Unlike churning, unauthorized trading may occur sporadically and without a pattern, making detection more challenging for investors.

The Anatomy of Unauthorized Trading

Unauthorized trading often stems from a breach of trust between investors and brokers. In some cases, brokers may act recklessly or maliciously, disregarding established protocols and guidelines governing client accounts. Alternatively, unauthorized trading may result from miscommunication or misunderstanding between investors and brokers regarding investment strategies and objectives.

Red Flags and Warning Signs

Investors should remain vigilant for red flags signaling potential unauthorized trading activity. These may include unexplained fluctuations in account balances, unfamiliar securities holdings, and discrepancies between executed trades and investor instructions. Promptly addressing any discrepancies or irregularities with brokers can help mitigate the impact of unauthorized trading and safeguard investor interests.

Legal Recourse and Remedies

In the event of unauthorized trading, investors possess legal recourse to seek restitution and hold accountable those responsible for the unauthorized activity. Securities laws afford investors the right to pursue civil litigation against brokers who engage in unauthorized trading, seeking damages for financial losses incurred as a result of the misconduct. Additionally, regulatory bodies may impose sanctions and disciplinary measures against brokers found to have violated securities regulations.

Conclusion

Churning and unauthorized trading represent egregious violations of investor trust, undermining the integrity of financial markets and jeopardizing the financial well-being of investors. By understanding the mechanisms and consequences of these fraudulent practices, investors can empower themselves to detect and prevent exploitation by unscrupulous brokers. Through enhanced transparency, regulatory oversight, and investor education, we can strive to foster a climate of trust and accountability within the financial industry, ensuring the protection of investor interests and the preservation of market integrity.

Introduction

Financial frauds and scams have plagued societies for centuries, preying on the vulnerable and unsuspecting. Among the most notorious of these schemes is the pyramid scheme, a deceptive and often destructive model that promises riches but ultimately leaves its participants in ruin. In this article, we will delve into the structure of pyramid schemes, examining how they operate, why they are so insidious, and how individuals can protect themselves from falling victim to their allure.

Understanding Pyramid Schemes

At its core, a pyramid scheme is a fraudulent investment scheme that generates returns for early investors by recruiting new investors. The structure resembles a pyramid, with a single individual or a small group at the top reaping the majority of the profits, while those at the bottom struggle to recoup their investments. The success of the scheme relies heavily on recruiting new members rather than selling a legitimate product or service.

The Pyramid Scheme Structure

Pyramid schemes typically operate under the guise of a legitimate business opportunity or investment program. The initial investors, often referred to as "founders" or "promoters", entice others to join by promising high returns or extravagant rewards for minimal effort. These promises are rarely fulfilled, as the scheme depends on an ever-expanding base of recruits to sustain itself.

As new participants join the scheme, they are required to make an initial investment or purchase a starter kit, product, or service. A portion of this investment is then funneled up the pyramid to the individuals at the top, while the rest may be used to pay returns to earlier investors or to further promote the scheme through advertising and recruitment efforts.

The Cycle of Deception

One of the key characteristics of pyramid schemes is their inherent instability. As the scheme grows, the pool of potential recruits dwindles, making it increasingly difficult for new investors to recover their initial investments. Eventually, the scheme collapses under its own weight, leaving the majority of participants with significant financial losses.

The individuals who benefit most from pyramid schemes are often those who initiate them or join early on. By leveraging their position at the top of the pyramid, they stand to gain substantial profits at the expense of those who join later. Meanwhile, participants further down the pyramid are left with little to show for their investments, having been lured by false promises of wealth and prosperity.

Legal and Ethical Implications

Pyramid schemes are not only financially ruinous but also illegal in many jurisdictions. Most countries have laws in place that prohibit schemes that rely primarily on recruitment rather than the sale of a genuine product or service. Despite these regulations, pyramid schemes continue to proliferate, often operating under the radar or disguising themselves as legitimate multi-level marketing (MLM) programs.

Distinguishing Between MLMs and Pyramid Schemes

While MLMs share some similarities with pyramid schemes, there are key differences that set them apart. Unlike pyramid schemes, legitimate MLMs derive their revenue primarily from the sale of products or services to end consumers, rather than from recruitment fees or investments. Participants in MLMs earn commissions based on the sales they generate, rather than solely from recruiting new members.

However, distinguishing between MLMs and pyramid schemes can be challenging, as some schemes may attempt to mask their true nature by emphasizing product sales while still prioritizing recruitment as the primary source of income. In such cases, it is essential for individuals to conduct thorough research and exercise caution before investing time or money in any business opportunity.

Protecting Yourself Against Pyramid Schemes

Educating oneself about the characteristics of pyramid schemes is the first step in protecting against falling victim to financial fraud. Some key red flags to watch out for include:

- ❖ Promises of high returns with little or no risk.
- ❖ Emphasis on recruitment over the sale of legitimate products or services.
- ❖ Lack of transparency regarding the company's business model or financials.
- ❖ Pressure to recruit friends and family members.

❖ Difficulty in obtaining clear answers to questions about the business opportunity.

In addition to recognizing these warning signs, individuals should also be wary of any investment opportunity that seems too good to be true. Conducting thorough due diligence, seeking advice from financial professionals, and avoiding impulsive decisions can help mitigate the risk of falling prey to pyramid schemes and other fraudulent schemes.

Conclusion

Pyramid schemes represent a pervasive and persistent threat to individuals seeking financial security and prosperity. By understanding the structure of these schemes, recognizing the warning signs, and exercising caution when evaluating investment opportunities, individuals can protect themselves from falling victim to financial fraud. As awareness of pyramid schemes grows and regulatory agencies continue to crack down on fraudulent activities, individuals must remain vigilant in safeguarding their hard-earned assets against exploitation and deception. Through education, diligence, and informed decision-making, we can collectively work towards a future where financial fraud is no longer a barrier to economic empowerment and success.

Introduction

Financial frauds and scams have plagued economies for centuries, leaving a trail of devastation in their wake. Among the myriad forms of financial deception, Ponzi schemes stand out as one of the most infamous and damaging. Originating from the schemes devised by Charles Ponzi in the early 20th century, Ponzi schemes have evolved and persisted, ensnaring unsuspecting investors in their web of deceit. This article delves into the history, mechanics, and notorious cases of Ponzi schemes, shedding light on their intricacies and the devastation they wreak on individuals and economies alike.

The Genesis of Ponzi Schemes

Ponzi schemes trace their origins to Charles Ponzi, an Italian immigrant who operated one of the most infamous financial frauds in history during the early 1920s. Ponzi promised investors lucrative returns by exploiting discrepancies in international postal reply coupons. His scheme involved using new investors' funds to pay returns to earlier investors, creating an illusion of profitability while siphoning off funds for personal gain. The scheme eventually collapsed, leading to Ponzi's arrest and imprisonment. Despite its ignominious end, Ponzi's scheme set a precedent for future fraudsters seeking to exploit investor greed and ignorance.

Mechanics of Ponzi Schemes

At their core, Ponzi schemes operate on a simple premise: promise high returns with little to no risk. The mechanics typically involve enticing investors with the prospect of quick and exorbitant profits, often through non-existent or unsustainable ventures. Initially, early investors may receive the promised returns, creating a veneer of legitimacy and attracting more capital. However, instead of generating profits through legitimate means, Ponzi operators use incoming funds to pay returns to existing investors, perpetuating the cycle of deception. As the scheme grows, the operator must continually recruit new investors to sustain payouts, inevitably leading to collapse when the influx of new funds dwindles or authorities intervene.

Psychological Dynamics

Ponzi schemes thrive on a combination of deception and psychology, exploiting investors' greed, ignorance, and trust. The promise of high returns in a short period triggers irrational exuberance, blinding investors to warning signs and red flags. Additionally, Ponzi operators often cultivate an aura of exclusivity and secrecy, fostering a sense of belonging and trust among participants. Moreover, the fear of missing out (FOMO) compels individuals to invest hastily without conducting due diligence or questioning the scheme's sustainability. By preying on these psychological vulnerabilities, Ponzi schemes ensnare individuals from all walks of life, perpetuating their cycle of deception.

Notorious Cases of Ponzi Schemes

Throughout history, Ponzi schemes have left a trail of devastation, ruining lives and fortunes in their wake. Among the most notorious cases include:

1. Bernard Madoff's Ponzi Scheme

Perhaps the most infamous Ponzi scheme in modern history, Bernard Madoff's fraudulent scheme operated for over two decades, defrauding investors of billions of dollars. Madoff, a respected figure on Wall Street, lured investors with the promise of steady, high returns through his investment advisory firm. However, instead of investing funds as promised, Madoff used new investors' money to pay returns to existing clients while siphoning off millions for personal gain. The scheme collapsed in 2008 amid the financial crisis, leading to Madoff's arrest and eventual conviction.

2. The Stanford Financial Group

Allen Stanford's eponymous financial empire collapsed in 2009 following revelations of a massive Ponzi scheme. Stanford, a flamboyant financier, enticed investors with promises of high returns through certificates of deposit (CDs) issued by his bank in Antigua. In reality, Stanford misappropriated billions of dollars to fund his lavish lifestyle and speculative ventures. The scheme unraveled when the global financial crisis exposed its unsustainable nature, resulting in Stanford's arrest and conviction on multiple counts of fraud.

Originating in Russia during the early 1990s, the MMM Ponzi scheme orchestrated by Sergei Mavrodi ranks among the largest financial frauds in history. Mavrodi promised investors astronomical returns through a pyramid scheme that purportedly invested in stocks, real estate, and other ventures. However, the scheme relied on recruiting new investors to pay returns to existing participants, leading to its eventual collapse in 1994. Despite Mavrodi's arrest and imprisonment, the MMM scheme left millions of investors bankrupt and disillusioned.

Regulatory Challenges and Mitigation Efforts

Despite regulatory oversight and enforcement measures, Ponzi schemes continue to proliferate, exploiting regulatory loopholes and evolving tactics to evade detection. Regulatory agencies face challenges in detecting and preventing Ponzi schemes, given their clandestine nature and the complexities of modern financial markets. Moreover, the global nature of Ponzi schemes poses jurisdictional challenges, hindering coordinated efforts to combat fraud. However, regulatory reforms, enhanced transparency, and investor education initiatives are critical in mitigating the risks posed by Ponzi schemes and protecting investors from financial exploitation.

Conclusion

Ponzi schemes represent a dark underbelly of the financial world, preying on human greed and gullibility to perpetrate deception and fraud. From Charles Ponzi to modern-day fraudsters, the allure of easy money continues to entice individuals into schemes with devastating consequences. By understanding the history, mechanics, and notorious cases of Ponzi schemes, investors can arm themselves with knowledge to identify red flags and protect their hard-earned assets from financial predators. Moreover, regulatory vigilance, transparency, and investor education are essential in safeguarding against future Ponzi schemes and preserving trust and integrity in financial markets.

High-Yield Investment Scams

Introduction

In the realm of finance, the allure of high-yield investments has always captivated investors seeking quick and substantial returns on their capital. However, amidst legitimate investment opportunities, a darker underbelly lurks – high-yield investment scams. These schemes promise extraordinary returns with minimal risk, exploiting the vulnerability and greed of unsuspecting investors. In this article, we delve into the anatomy of high-yield investment scams, unraveling their deceptive tactics and cautionary tales.

Understanding High-Yield Investment Scams

High-yield investment scams typically operate under the guise of legitimate investment vehicles, promising outsized returns that far exceed market norms. Commonly known as "get-rich-quick" schemes, these fraudulent endeavors prey on individuals who are enticed by the prospect of effortless wealth accumulation. They often leverage sophisticated marketing tactics, enticing investors with glossy brochures, persuasive sales pitches, and testimonials from purportedly satisfied clients. However, beneath the façade of legitimacy lies a web of deceit and manipulation orchestrated by unscrupulous operators.

The Illusion of Guaranteed Returns

One of the hallmarks of high-yield investment scams is the promise of guaranteed returns, regardless of market conditions. Fraudulent operators exploit investors' desire for financial security by assuring them of consistent profits, irrespective of prevailing economic realities. However, in the world of legitimate investments, guaranteed returns are virtually non-existent, as market fluctuations and unforeseen events can impact investment performance. By peddling the illusion of guaranteed returns, scam artists lure unsuspecting investors into a false sense of security, setting the stage for financial ruin.

Complex Investment Structures

High-yield investment scams often employ complex investment structures to obfuscate their fraudulent activities and deter scrutiny. These schemes may involve convoluted arrangements such as Ponzi schemes, pyramid schemes, or offshore accounts, making it challenging for investors to discern the true nature of their investments. Moreover, scam operators may use sophisticated financial jargon and false documentation to create an aura of legitimacy, further deceiving investors who lack the necessary expertise to evaluate the intricacies of the investment.

Lack of Regulatory Oversight

One of the significant challenges in combating high-yield investment scams is the lack of robust regulatory oversight in certain jurisdictions. Many fraudulent schemes operate in regions with lax regulatory frameworks or inadequate enforcement mechanisms, allowing scam operators to perpetrate their illicit activities with impunity. In the absence of stringent regulatory oversight, investors are left vulnerable to exploitation, as fraudulent operators continue to exploit legal loopholes and evade accountability.

Red Flags and Warning Signs

While high-yield investment scams may appear enticing on the surface, there are several red flags and warning signs that investors should be vigilant of.

1. Unrealistic Returns: Be wary of investment opportunities that promise consistently high returns with minimal risk, as genuine investment returns are typically commensurate with market performance.

2. Lack of Transparency: If an investment opportunity lacks transparency regarding its underlying assets, investment strategy, or operational structure, it may be indicative of fraudulent activity.

3. Pressure to Invest Quickly: Scam operators often employ high-pressure sales tactics to compel investors to make hasty investment decisions without conducting proper due diligence.

4. Unsolicited Offers: Exercise caution when approached with unsolicited investment offers via cold calls (unsolicited telephone calls made to potential customers without prior contact or permission), emails, or social media messages, as legitimate investment opportunities are rarely solicited in such manner.

Case Studies and Real-Life Examples

To illustrate the perils of high-yield investment scams, we examine notable case studies and real-life examples.

1. Bernie Madoff Ponzi Scheme: Perhaps one of the most infamous investment scams in history, Bernie Madoff's Ponzi scheme defrauded investors of billions of dollars by

promising consistently high returns through fictitious investment strategies.

2. Bitconnect: Bitconnect, a cryptocurrency lending platform, collapsed in 2018 amidst allegations of operating a Ponzi scheme. Investors suffered substantial losses as the platform's promised returns proved unsustainable, highlighting the risks associated with unregulated digital assets.

3. Woodbridge Group of Companies: The Woodbridge Group of Companies orchestrated a massive real estate investment scheme, promising investors high returns through purported real estate investments. However, the scheme collapsed in 2017, leading to bankruptcy filings and legal proceedings against the company's executives.

Conclusion

High-yield investment scams represent a pervasive threat to investors seeking to grow their wealth through legitimate means. As financial markets evolve and new investment opportunities emerge, it is imperative for investors to exercise diligence and skepticism when evaluating potential investment opportunities. By educating themselves about the warning signs of investment scams and conducting thorough due diligence, investors can mitigate the risk of falling victim to fraudulent schemes. Ultimately, the pursuit of financial prosperity should be guided by prudence, integrity, and a commitment to ethical investing practices.

Introduction

In the realm of finance, transparency and integrity are paramount. However, amidst the complexity of financial transactions and services, there lies a nefarious practice known as fee padding. Fee padding involves the addition of hidden charges and unethical practices by financial institutions, often to the detriment of unsuspecting consumers. This article delves into the insidious nature of fee padding, exploring its various forms, implications, and ways to safeguard against such fraudulent practices.

Understanding Fee Padding

Fee padding, also referred to as fee inflation, is the deliberate act of adding excessive or undisclosed fees to financial transactions, products, or services. While fees are a legitimate aspect of many financial transactions, padding them with additional and often unjustified charges crosses ethical boundaries. These hidden fees can manifest in various forms, including maintenance fees, service charges, transaction fees, and administrative costs.

Forms of Fee Padding

1. Maintenance Fees and Account Charges

Financial institutions often impose maintenance fees or account charges under the guise of covering operational costs. However, these fees can be excessive and disproportionate to the services provided. Customers may find themselves paying monthly maintenance fees for basic banking services, eroding their savings over time.

2. Transaction Fees and Service Charges

Transactions, such as wire transfers, ATM withdrawals, and foreign currency exchanges, are fertile ground for fee padding. Financial institutions may levy inflated transaction fees and service charges, often without transparent disclosure. These hidden costs can significantly diminish the value of financial transactions and investments.

3. Administrative Costs and Overhead Charges

Behind the scenes, administrative costs and overhead charges can contribute to fee padding. These expenses, purportedly incurred for processing, documentation, and regulatory compliance, are sometimes inflated to bolster profits at the expense of customers.

Implications of Fee Padding

The prevalence of fee padding poses significant ramifications for consumers and the integrity of financial markets.

1. Financial Burden on Consumers

Fee padding places an undue financial burden on consumers, particularly those with limited resources. Hidden charges diminish the purchasing power of individuals and families, making it challenging to achieve financial stability and meet essential needs.

2. Erosion of Trust and Credibility

Fee padding undermines trust and credibility in financial institutions and the broader financial ecosystem. When consumers discover hidden charges and unethical practices, it erodes confidence in the integrity of the financial sector, leading to diminished trust and loyalty.

3. Barrier to Financial Inclusion

For marginalized and underserved communities, fee padding exacerbates barriers to financial inclusion. High fees and hidden charges deter individuals from accessing basic banking services and participating in the formal financial system, perpetuating economic inequality.

Safeguarding Against Fee Padding

To protect consumers and mitigate the risk of fee padding, proactive measures and regulatory interventions are essential.

1. Enhanced Transparency and Disclosure

Financial institutions should prioritize transparency and disclosure regarding fees and charges associated with their products and services. Clear and comprehensible communication empowers consumers to make informed decisions and hold institutions accountable for their pricing practices.

2. Regulatory Oversight and Enforcement

Regulators play a crucial role in monitoring and enforcing compliance with consumer protection laws and regulations. Robust oversight mechanisms are necessary to detect and deter fee padding, imposing sanctions and penalties on institutions found engaging in unethical practices.

3. Consumer Education and Advocacy

Empowering consumers with financial literacy and advocacy resources is instrumental in combatting fee padding. Educational initiatives raise awareness about common fee structures, rights and responsibilities as consumers, and avenues for recourse in cases of fee padding and financial fraud.

Conclusion

Fee padding represents a pervasive threat to financial transparency, fairness, and consumer welfare. By understanding the forms and implications of fee padding, stakeholders can work together to combat unethical practices and uphold the principles of integrity and accountability in the financial sector. Through enhanced transparency, regulatory oversight, and consumer empowerment, we can mitigate the risks posed by fee padding and foster a more equitable and trustworthy financial ecosystem.

Introduction

Mortgage fraud represents a complex web of deceitful practices within the real estate financing sector, causing significant financial losses and legal repercussions. With the soaring demand for homeownership and the lucrative nature of real estate transactions, perpetrators exploit vulnerabilities in the mortgage process, perpetrating various forms of fraud. This article delves into the intricacies of mortgage fraud, exploring its types, causes, impacts, and preventive measures.

Understanding Mortgage Fraud

Mortgage fraud encompasses a spectrum of illicit activities aimed at deceiving lenders, borrowers, and other stakeholders involved in real estate transactions. It involves misrepresentation, falsification, or omission of information to obtain a mortgage loan under false pretenses. Perpetrators manipulate documents, inflate property values, and engage in other deceptive tactics to secure financing unlawfully.

Types of Mortgage Fraud

1. Application Fraud: Perpetrators provide false or misleading information on mortgage applications to qualify for loans they would otherwise not be eligible for. This includes misrepresenting income, assets, employment history, and liabilities.

2. Property Fraud: Inflating the value of properties through fraudulent appraisals or falsified documentation to obtain larger loans or cash-out refinancing.

3. Occupancy Fraud: Borrowers misrepresent their intent to occupy the property as their primary residence when, in reality, they intend to use it for investment purposes or rent it out.

4. Employment Fraud: Falsifying employment records or creating fictitious companies to fabricate stable income streams and enhance loan eligibility.

5. Identity Fraud: Stealing or fabricating identities to apply for mortgage loans without the consent or knowledge of the legitimate individuals.

6. Foreclosure Rescue Scams: Exploiting financially distressed homeowners by promising foreclosure assistance in exchange for upfront fees or the transfer of property titles.

Causes of Mortgage Fraud

1. Economic Pressures: Economic downturns and financial hardships can drive individuals to commit mortgage fraud to alleviate financial burdens or maintain a lavish lifestyle.

2. Inadequate Oversight: Weak regulatory oversight and lax enforcement facilitate fraudulent activities within the mortgage industry, allowing perpetrators to exploit loopholes and evade detection.

3. Mortgage Industry Practices: Pressure to meet lending quotas and generate profits can incentivize mortgage

professionals to turn a blind eye to suspicious activities or actively participate in fraudulent schemes.

4. Complex Transactions: The complexity of real estate transactions and the multitude of parties involved create opportunities for fraudsters to manipulate documents and conceal illicit activities.

Impacts of Mortgage Fraud

Mortgage fraud imposes far-reaching consequences on individuals, financial institutions, and the broader economy.

1. Financial Losses: Victims of mortgage fraud incur financial losses resulting from unpaid loans, inflated property values, and legal expenses associated with pursuing legal recourse.

2. Erosion of Trust: Mortgage fraud undermines trust in the integrity of the real estate market and financial institutions, tarnishing their reputations and eroding investor confidence.

3. Legal Ramifications: Perpetrators of mortgage fraud face civil lawsuits, criminal charges, and imprisonment upon conviction, facing severe penalties for their illicit actions.

4. Economic Instability: Widespread mortgage fraud can destabilize housing markets, trigger foreclosures, and contribute to economic downturns, posing systemic risks to the financial system.

Preventive Measures against Mortgage Fraud

1. Strengthening Regulatory Oversight: Regulators must implement robust oversight mechanisms, conduct regular audits, and enforce stringent compliance standards to detect and deter mortgage fraud.

2. Enhanced Due Diligence: Lenders should conduct thorough due diligence on loan applications, verify borrower information, and scrutinize property valuations to mitigate the risk of fraud.

3. Investing in Technology: Embracing technology-driven solutions such as artificial intelligence, machine learning, and data analytics can enhance fraud detection capabilities and identify suspicious patterns in mortgage transactions.

4. Educating Stakeholders: Educating borrowers, lenders, and real estate professionals about the warning signs of mortgage fraud and the consequences of engaging in fraudulent activities can foster greater awareness and vigilance.

5. Collaboration and Information Sharing: Encouraging collaboration among industry stakeholders, law enforcement agencies, and regulatory bodies can facilitate the exchange of information and intelligence to combat mortgage fraud effectively.

Conclusion

Mortgage fraud remains a pervasive threat to the integrity of the real estate financing sector, posing significant financial, legal, and reputational risks to stakeholders. By understanding the various forms of mortgage fraud, addressing underlying causes, and implementing proactive measures, industry participants can safeguard against fraudulent activities and uphold the integrity of the mortgage lending process. Vigilance, transparency, and collaboration are essential in combating mortgage fraud and preserving the stability of the housing market and financial system.

Introduction

In today's digital age, where technology permeates every aspect of our lives, the risk of financial frauds and scams looms larger than ever. Among the myriad forms of cybercrime, identity theft and phishing scams stand out as particularly pervasive and damaging. Understanding these threats and adopting proactive measures to mitigate risks are essential for safeguarding personal and financial information in the digital realm.

Understanding Identity Theft

Identity theft occurs when a malicious actor gains unauthorized access to an individual's personal information and uses it for fraudulent purposes. This stolen information typically includes sensitive data such as social security numbers, credit card details, bank account information, and passwords. Perpetrators employ various methods to acquire this data, including data breaches, malware, social engineering tactics, and even dumpster diving (searching through trash).

The consequences of identity theft can be devastating for victims, extending beyond financial losses to include damage to credit scores, legal complications, and emotional distress. Moreover, the effects may not be immediately apparent, as identity thieves often operate stealthily, exploiting stolen information over an extended period.

The Anatomy of Phishing Scams

Phishing scams represent another prevalent form of cyber fraud wherein attackers impersonate legitimate entities to deceive individuals into divulging sensitive information or performing actions that compromise security. Phishing attacks typically manifest through emails, text messages, or phone calls that appear authentic, luring recipients into clicking on malicious links, downloading malware-infected attachments, or disclosing confidential data.

Phishing tactics continue to evolve, becoming increasingly sophisticated and difficult to detect. From elaborate email spoofing to convincing replicas of trusted websites, perpetrators employ psychological manipulation and social engineering techniques to exploit human vulnerabilities and elicit desired responses from unsuspecting victims.

Recognizing Red Flags

Recognizing the warning signs of identity theft and phishing scams is paramount for preemptive action. Common indicators include unsolicited requests for personal information, grammatical errors and inconsistencies in communication, suspicious URLs and email addresses, and urgent demands for immediate action. Additionally, scrutinizing financial statements regularly and monitoring credit reports can help detect unauthorized transactions and potential signs of fraudulent activity.

Education and awareness play pivotal roles in fortifying defenses against cyber threats. By staying informed about prevalent scams and cultivating a healthy skepticism towards unsolicited communications, individuals can bolster their resilience against malicious actors seeking to exploit vulnerabilities in the digital ecosystem.

Mitigating Risks and Enhancing Security

Mitigating the risks of identity theft and phishing scams requires a multi-faceted approach that encompasses technological solutions, behavioral adjustments, and proactive risk management strategies. Implementing robust cybersecurity measures such as firewalls, encryption protocols, and anti-malware software can fortify digital defenses and thwart malicious intrusions.

Furthermore, practicing good cyber hygiene habits, such as using strong, unique passwords, enabling two-factor authentication, and exercising caution when sharing personal information online, can significantly reduce susceptibility to cyber threats. Regularly updating software and operating systems also helps patch vulnerabilities and safeguard against emerging security risks.

Empowering Individuals and Communities

Beyond individual efforts, fostering a culture of cybersecurity awareness within communities and organizations is essential for combating the pervasive threat of digital fraud. Education initiatives, cybersecurity training programs, and collaborative information-sharing platforms can empower individuals with the knowledge and resources needed to navigate the digital landscape safely.

Moreover, advocating for legislative measures and industry standards that prioritize consumer protection and data privacy can strengthen regulatory frameworks and hold perpetrators of financial frauds and scams accountable for their actions. By fostering a collective commitment to cybersecurity, we can foster a safer and more resilient digital ecosystem for future generations.

Conclusion

Identity theft and phishing scams represent formidable challenges in an increasingly interconnected and digitized world. As technology continues to advance, so too must our vigilance and preparedness in combating cyber threats. By understanding the mechanisms of digital fraud, recognizing red flags, and adopting proactive measures to enhance security, individuals can safeguard their personal and financial information from malicious actors seeking to exploit vulnerabilities for illicit gain.

In the ever-evolving landscape of financial frauds and scams, education, awareness, and collaborative action are our most potent weapons. By working together to foster a culture of cybersecurity and resilience, we can navigate the digital frontier with confidence and protect the integrity of our identities and financial well-being for generations to come.

Introduction

In the digital age, financial institutions face an unprecedented challenge: the constant threat of cybersecurity breaches. With the increasing reliance on technology for banking, investing, and transactions, the financial sector has become a prime target for cybercriminals seeking to exploit vulnerabilities and gain unauthorized access to sensitive information. In this article, we delve into the complexities of cybersecurity breaches in financial institutions, exploring the vulnerabilities that expose them to risk and the severe consequences that follow such breaches.

Understanding Cybersecurity Vulnerabilities

Financial institutions, including banks, investment firms, and insurance companies, store vast amounts of sensitive data, including customer information, financial records, and transaction histories. This treasure trove of data makes them attractive targets for cyber attackers seeking to steal valuable information for financial gain or to disrupt operations for malicious purposes.

Insider Threats

One of the most significant vulnerabilities faced by financial institutions is the insider threat. Employees with access to sensitive systems and information can inadvertently or maliciously compromise security measures, leading to data breaches or financial fraud. Whether through negligence, coercion, or disgruntlement, insiders pose a significant risk that financial institutions must address through robust access controls, employee training, and continuous monitoring.

Phishing and Social Engineering

Cybercriminals often employ sophisticated tactics such as phishing and social engineering to trick employees or customers into divulging confidential information or installing malware. Phishing emails, for example, may mimic legitimate communications from banks or financial institutions, prompting recipients to click on malicious links or provide login credentials unknowingly. Similarly, social engineering techniques exploit human psychology to manipulate individuals into revealing sensitive information or performing actions that compromise security.

Weak Authentication Mechanisms

Inadequate authentication mechanisms, such as weak passwords or outdated authentication protocols, can leave financial institutions vulnerable to unauthorized access. Cyber attackers may exploit these weaknesses to gain entry into systems or accounts, bypassing security measures and gaining unrestricted access to sensitive data. Implementing multi-factor authentication, encryption, and biometric authentication can enhance security and mitigate the risk of unauthorized access.

Vulnerabilities in Third-Party Systems

Financial institutions often rely on third-party vendors and service providers for various functions, including payment processing, data storage, and software solutions. However, these third-party systems may introduce additional vulnerabilities and security risks, as they may not adhere to the same rigorous security standards as the financial institution itself. Failure to adequately assess and monitor the security posture of third-party vendors can expose financial institutions to significant risks and potential breaches.

Consequences of Cybersecurity Breaches

The consequences of cybersecurity breaches in financial institutions can be far-reaching, encompassing financial losses, reputational damage, regulatory scrutiny, and legal liabilities. When sensitive information falls into the wrong hands or systems are compromised, the repercussions can be severe and long-lasting.

Financial Losses

Cybersecurity breaches can result in substantial financial losses for financial institutions, stemming from theft of funds, fraudulent transactions, and operational disruptions. In addition to direct financial losses, institutions may incur costs associated with incident response, forensic investigations, and remediation efforts to restore systems and mitigate future risks. Moreover, the impact of a breach on customer trust and confidence can lead to revenue loss as customers may take their business elsewhere in search of more secure alternatives.

Reputational Damage

The trust and confidence of customers are paramount in the financial industry. However, a cybersecurity breach can shatter that trust and inflict lasting damage to the reputation of a financial institution. News of a data breach or security incident can spread rapidly through traditional and social media channels, tarnishing the institution's image and eroding customer loyalty. Rebuilding trust and restoring reputation in the aftermath of a breach can be a formidable challenge that requires transparent communication, proactive measures, and tangible improvements to cybersecurity practices.

Regulatory Scrutiny and Compliance Penalties

Financial institutions operate within a highly regulated environment governed by stringent cybersecurity and data protection regulations. In the event of a breach, regulatory authorities may launch investigations to assess the institution's compliance with applicable laws and regulations, including the General Data Protection Regulation (GDPR) in the Eurpean Union, the Payment Card Industry Data Security Standard (PCI DSS), and the Sarbanes-Oxley Act (SOX) in the United States. Non-compliance with regulatory requirements can result in significant fines, penalties, and sanctions, further exacerbating the financial and reputational impact of a breach.

Legal Liabilities and Lawsuits

Cybersecurity breaches can expose financial institutions to legal liabilities and lawsuits from affected parties, including customers, shareholders, and regulatory bodies. Victims of data breaches may seek damages for identity theft, financial fraud, and other harms resulting from the unauthorized disclosure of their personal information. Class-action lawsuits (legal actions filed by a group of individuals collectively representing a larger class who have been similarly harmed or wronged by a defendant) and regulatory enforcement actions can result in substantial legal costs, settlements, and judgments, imposing a heavy financial burden on the institution and its stakeholders.

Conclusion

Cybersecurity breaches pose a significant and evolving threat to financial institutions, requiring constant vigilance, proactive measures, and robust security controls to mitigate risks and safeguard sensitive information. By understanding the vulnerabilities that expose them to cyber threats and the severe consequences that follow such breaches, financial institutions can enhance their resilience, strengthen their defenses, and protect the interests of their customers, shareholders, and stakeholders in an increasingly digital world.

Introduction

Money laundering is a pervasive and complex issue that permeates the global financial system, posing significant challenges to regulatory authorities, law enforcement agencies, and financial institutions alike. It represents a critical component of many illicit activities, including drug trafficking, terrorism financing, corruption, and organized crime. Understanding the mechanisms, impacts, and countermeasures of money laundering is essential for safeguarding the integrity of the financial system and combating financial frauds and scams effectively.

The Nature of Money Laundering

Money laundering is the process of disguising the origins of illegally obtained money, typically through a series of complex transactions, to make it appear legitimate. The primary objective is to integrate illicit funds into the mainstream economy without arousing suspicion or attracting regulatory scrutiny. This clandestine activity enables criminals to enjoy the proceeds of their crimes while evading detection and prosecution.

Stages of Money Laundering

Money laundering typically involves three distinct stages: placement, layering, and integration. During the placement stage, illicit funds are introduced into the financial system, often through cash deposits, currency exchanges, or investments in high-value assets. This initial step aims to distance the illicit proceeds from their criminal origins and facilitate their entry into legitimate channels.

In the layering stage, the launderers employ a variety of sophisticated techniques to obfuscate the trail of illicit funds and sever their connection to the underlying criminal activity. This may involve transferring funds between multiple accounts, conducting complex financial transactions, or routing them through offshore jurisdictions with lax regulatory oversight. The objective is to create a complex web of transactions that confounds investigators and masks the illicit source of the funds.

Finally, in the integration stage, the laundered funds are reintroduced into the economy as seemingly legitimate assets or investments. By acquiring tangible assets, such as real estate, luxury goods, or businesses, the launderers seek to legitimize their ill-gotten gains and enjoy the benefits of their criminal activities without fear of detection or prosecution.

Methods of Money Laundering

Money launderers employ a wide array of methods and techniques to conceal the illicit origins of their funds and evade detection by law enforcement authorities. Some common methods include:

1. Structuring: Also known as smurfing, this involves breaking down large sums of illicit cash into smaller, less conspicuous transactions to avoid triggering reporting requirements and arouse suspicion.

2. Trade-based Money Laundering: Criminals exploit international trade transactions to disguise the movement of illicit funds by manipulating invoices, misrepresenting the

value of goods, or engaging in over- and under-invoicing schemes.

3. Shell Companies: Launderers often establish shell companies, which exist only on paper and have no legitimate business activities, to obscure the ownership and movement of funds through a complex network of corporate structures and offshore accounts.

4. Real Estate Investments: Purchasing real estate assets with illicit funds provides money launderers with a means to legitimize their wealth while simultaneously concealing the proceeds of their criminal activities behind layers of legal and financial complexity.

5. Cryptocurrencies: The rise of cryptocurrencies has facilitated anonymous and untraceable transactions, making them an attractive vehicle for money laundering and illicit financial activities on a global scale.

The Impacts of Money Laundering

The pervasive nature of money laundering poses significant economic, social, and security risks to societies around the world. By enabling criminals to profit from illegal activities and evade accountability, money laundering undermines the integrity of financial institutions, erodes public trust in the rule of law, and distorts market dynamics.

Furthermore, money laundering has far-reaching consequences beyond financial markets, fueling corruption, destabilizing economies, and funding terrorist organizations and transnational criminal networks. The illicit proceeds laundered through the financial system perpetuate cycles of violence, exploitation, and inequality, exacerbating social tensions and undermining efforts to promote peace, stability, and sustainable development.

Combatting Money Laundering

To address the growing threat of money laundering, governments, regulatory authorities, and international organizations have implemented a range of regulatory frameworks, legislative measures, and enforcement mechanisms designed to detect, deter, and disrupt illicit financial activities.

Key initiatives include the implementation of anti-money laundering (AML) and counter-terrorism financing (CTF) laws, enhanced due diligence requirements for financial institutions, and the establishment of financial intelligence units (FIUs) tasked with analyzing suspicious transaction reports and disseminating actionable intelligence to law enforcement agencies.

Furthermore, international cooperation and information sharing among jurisdictions have become essential components of efforts to combat money laundering and enhance the effectiveness of cross-border investigations and prosecutions. Initiatives such as the Financial Action Task Force (FATF) provide a platform for collaboration and coordination among member states to strengthen AML/CFT standards and promote global adherence to best practices in combating financial crime.

Challenges and Emerging Trends

Despite significant progress in strengthening AML/CFT regimes and enhancing international cooperation, money laundering remains a persistent and evolving threat to the integrity of the global financial system. Rapid technological advancements, the proliferation of virtual assets, and the increasing interconnectedness of financial markets have created new opportunities and challenges for money launderers, requiring policymakers and regulators to adapt and innovate in response to emerging threats.

Moreover, the emergence of decentralized finance (DeFi) platforms, peer-to-peer networks, and anonymous cryptocurrencies presents unique challenges for traditional AML/CFT frameworks, as these innovative technologies offer new avenues for illicit actors to launder money and conceal their identities in cyberspace. *Decentralized finance* (DeFi), refers to a system of financial applications and platforms built on blockchain technology that operate without central intermediaries, allowing for peer-to-peer transactions, lending, borrowing, and other financial services in a decentralized manner.

Conclusion

Money laundering represents a complex and multifaceted challenge that requires a coordinated and comprehensive response from governments, financial institutions, and civil society stakeholders. By understanding the nature, methods, and impacts of money laundering, stakeholders can develop effective strategies and countermeasures to disrupt illicit financial networks, safeguard the integrity of the financial system, and protect vulnerable communities from the harmful effects of financial frauds and scams.

Through sustained efforts to strengthen regulatory compliance, enhance international cooperation, and leverage technological innovations, we can collectively combat money laundering and advance the shared goals of financial transparency, integrity, and accountability in the global fight against financial frauds and scams.

Introduction

Financial fraud poses a significant threat to individuals, businesses, and economies worldwide. As financial markets evolve and technology advances, perpetrators find new ways to exploit vulnerabilities, making it imperative for regulators and enforcement agencies to keep pace. In this article, we delve into the regulatory challenges associated with combating financial fraud and explore the various enforcement efforts aimed at mitigating this pervasive threat.

Understanding Financial Fraud

Financial fraud encompasses a wide range of deceptive practices designed to illegally obtain funds or assets. It can manifest in various forms, including securities fraud, accounting fraud, insider trading, Ponzi schemes, money laundering, and identity theft. These fraudulent activities not only erode investor confidence but also undermine the integrity and stability of financial systems.

Regulatory Framework

A robust regulatory framework is fundamental to safeguarding financial markets and protecting investors from fraudulent schemes. Regulatory bodies such as the Securities and Exchange Commission (SEC) in the United States, the Financial Conduct Authority (FCA) in the United Kingdom, and the European Securities and Markets

Authority (ESMA) in the European Union play pivotal roles in overseeing securities exchanges, broker-dealers, investment advisers, and other market participants. Additionally, international organizations like the Financial Action Task Force (FATF) collaborate to combat money laundering and terrorist financing on a global scale.

Challenges in Regulation

Despite the existence of regulatory mechanisms, combating financial fraud presents multifaceted challenges. One significant obstacle is the rapid evolution of technology, which enables fraudsters to perpetrate sophisticated schemes across borders and jurisdictions. The anonymity afforded by cryptocurrencies and online platforms further complicates detection and enforcement efforts. Moreover, regulatory arbitrage and jurisdictional differences pose challenges in coordinating investigations and prosecuting offenders effectively.

Regulatory Response

In response to emerging threats, regulatory authorities have adopted proactive measures to enhance surveillance, detection, and enforcement capabilities. This includes leveraging advanced data analytics, artificial intelligence, and machine learning algorithms to identify suspicious patterns and anomalies in financial transactions. Moreover, regulatory bodies collaborate with law enforcement agencies and international partners to share intelligence and coordinate enforcement actions against transnational fraud networks.

Enforcement Efforts

Enforcement agencies play a pivotal role in deterring financial fraud and holding perpetrators accountable for their actions. The Department of Justice (DOJ) and the Securities and Exchange Commission (SEC) in the United States, the Serious Fraud Office (SFO) in the United Kingdom, and various state attorneys general are tasked with investigating and prosecuting individuals and organizations engaged in fraudulent activities. Civil and criminal penalties, including fines, disgorgement of ill-gotten gains, and imprisonment, serve as deterrents to would-be offenders.

Public Awareness and Education

Enhancing public awareness and financial literacy is essential in preventing individuals from falling victim to fraudulent schemes. Regulatory agencies, consumer advocacy groups, and industry associations collaborate to educate investors about common red flags and best practices for protecting their assets. By promoting transparency and accountability, stakeholders can empower individuals to make informed financial decisions and resist fraudulent solicitations.

Global Cooperation

Given the cross-border nature of financial fraud, international cooperation is paramount in combating this transnational threat. Bilateral and multilateral agreements facilitate the exchange of information and evidence across jurisdictions, enabling law enforcement agencies to pursue and prosecute offenders globally. Initiatives such as the Egmont Group of Financial Intelligence Units and INTERPOL's Financial Crimes unit facilitate collaboration and coordination among member states to disrupt illicit financial flows and dismantle criminal networks.

Emerging Trends and Future Challenges

As financial markets evolve, new trends and challenges continue to emerge, posing fresh risks to investors and regulators alike. The proliferation of digital assets, crowdfunding platforms, and decentralized finance (DeFi) ecosystems present regulatory challenges in ensuring investor protection and market integrity. Regulators must adapt swiftly to technological innovations and anticipate emerging threats to preemptively address vulnerabilities in the financial system.

Conclusion

Financial fraud remains a persistent threat that requires concerted efforts from regulators, enforcement agencies, and stakeholders worldwide. While regulatory challenges abound, proactive enforcement efforts and enhanced cooperation among international partners are critical in safeguarding financial markets and preserving investor trust. By fostering transparency, accountability, and vigilance, the financial community can collectively combat fraud and uphold the integrity of global financial systems.

Chapter 16. Protecting Yourself Against Financial Fraud
Tips and Strategies for Investors

Introduction

In a world where financial fraud is a persistent threat, investors must arm themselves with knowledge and strategies to safeguard their hard-earned money. Despite advancements in technology and regulatory efforts, financial fraud continues to evolve, posing significant risks to individuals and institutions alike. As the final chapter in our exploration of financial frauds and scams, let us delve into practical tips and effective strategies that investors can employ to protect themselves in an increasingly complex financial landscape.

Understanding the Threat Landscape

Before delving into specific strategies, it's crucial to understand the diverse forms of financial fraud that exist. From insider trading and securities fraud to pyramid schemes and identity theft, perpetrators employ a myriad of tactics to deceive investors and siphon funds illicitly. By familiarizing themselves with common schemes and red flags, investors can better detect and avoid potential threats to their financial well-being.

Research and Due Diligence

One of the most effective ways to mitigate the risk of falling victim to financial fraud is through thorough research and due diligence. Before making any investment decisions, investors should conduct comprehensive research on the investment opportunity, the individuals or entities involved, and the underlying fundamentals of the investment. This includes reviewing financial statements, assessing market conditions, and verifying the credentials of financial professionals or advisors.

Diversification and Risk Management

Diversification is a fundamental principle of investment strategy that can help mitigate the impact of financial fraud. By spreading investments across different asset classes, sectors, and geographical regions, investors can reduce their exposure to specific risks and minimize the potential impact of fraudulent activities targeting a single investment or sector. Additionally, implementing risk management techniques such as setting stop-loss orders and maintaining a balanced portfolio can help protect against sudden downturns and unexpected events.

Staying Informed and Vigilant

In today's fast-paced financial markets, staying informed and vigilant is essential for protecting against financial fraud. Investors should remain abreast of market developments, regulatory changes, and emerging trends that may impact their investments. This includes monitoring news sources, regulatory filings, and industry publications for relevant information and updates. By staying informed, investors can identify potential risks and take proactive measures to safeguard their investments.

Skepticism and Critical Thinking

Maintaining a healthy dose of skepticism and exercising critical thinking can also help investors avoid falling victim to financial fraud. While promises of high returns and guaranteed profits may be enticing, investors should approach such claims with caution and skepticism. It's essential to ask probing questions, scrutinize investment proposals, and seek independent verification before committing funds to any investment opportunity. By exercising discernment and critical thinking, investors can avoid being swayed by fraudulent schemes and deceptive practices.

Protecting Personal Information and Assets

In an era of increasing digital connectivity, protecting personal information and assets is paramount to guarding against identity theft and cyber fraud. Investors should take proactive measures to safeguard sensitive information such as bank account details, social security numbers, and login credentials. This includes using strong, unique passwords, enabling multi-factor authentication, and avoiding sharing personal information on insecure websites or platforms. Additionally, regularly monitoring financial statements and credit reports can help detect unauthorized activity and address potential security breaches promptly.

Seeking Professional Advice and Assistance

For investors navigating complex financial markets, seeking professional advice and assistance can provide valuable guidance and expertise. Working with qualified financial advisors, accountants, and legal professionals can help investors develop personalized investment strategies, navigate regulatory requirements, and address potential risks effectively. When selecting financial professionals, investors should prioritize individuals or firms with reputable credentials, industry experience, and a track record of ethical conduct.

Reporting Suspicious Activity

Finally, investors play a crucial role in combating financial fraud by reporting suspicious activity to the appropriate authorities. Whether encountering fraudulent investment schemes, suspicious transactions, or potential violations of securities laws, investors should not hesitate to report their concerns to regulatory agencies such as the Securities and Exchange Commission (SEC) or the Financial Industry Regulatory Authority (FINRA) in the United States. By reporting suspicious activity promptly, investors can contribute to the enforcement efforts aimed at deterring fraud and protecting the integrity of financial markets.

Conclusion

Protecting oneself against financial fraud requires vigilance, diligence, and informed decision-making. By understanding the threat landscape, conducting thorough research, staying informed, and exercising skepticism, investors can mitigate the risk of falling victim to fraudulent schemes and scams. Moreover, by implementing sound risk management practices, safeguarding personal information, seeking professional advice, and reporting suspicious activity, investors can proactively protect their financial interests and contribute to the integrity and transparency of financial markets. In an ever-evolving financial landscape, awareness and vigilance are the keys to safeguarding against financial fraud and preserving the trust and integrity of the investment ecosystem.

"Insights into Financial Frauds and Scams" delves deep into the intricate web of financial malfeasance, offering a comprehensive exploration of deceptive practices that plague markets worldwide. From the fundamental concepts in Chapter 1, which illuminate the landscape of financial fraud, to the insidious mechanisms of insider trading, securities fraud, and market manipulation detailed in subsequent chapters, this book provides invaluable insights into various forms of financial deceit.

With discussions on pyramid schemes, Ponzi schemes, identity theft, cybersecurity breaches, and regulatory challenges, readers gain a nuanced understanding of the multifaceted nature of financial fraud. Moreover, practical guidance in the concluding chapters equips investors with strategies to safeguard their assets. An indispensable resource for anyone navigating the complex terrain of finance, this book serves as a beacon of awareness and empowerment in the fight against financial fraud.

ABOUT THE AUTHOR

Mr. C. P. Kumar is a retired Scientist 'G' from National Institute of Hydrology, Roorkee, Uttarakhand, India. He is also a Reiki Healer and Chakra Balancing practitioner (with pendulum dowsing) and offers Emotional Freedom Technique (EFT) to help individuals with emotional issues. Mr. Kumar has authored many books on technical, spiritual, and social topics.

For further details, you may visit his webpage
https://www.angelfire.com/nh/cpkumar/virgo.html

www.ingramcontent.com/pod-product-compliance
Lightning Source LLC
Chambersburg PA
CBHW061620130726
47996CB00003B/1059